Sometimes THE HEART Must Speak

Sometimes the Heart Must Speak

POEMS TO ENCOURAGE AND ENLIGHTEN

FELECIA OKPAGU

Copyright © 2015 by Felecia Okpagu

All rights reserved. This book or any portion thereof may not be reproduced or used in any manner whatsoever without the express written permission of the publisher except for the use of brief quotations in a book review.

Scripture References noted (NIV) were taken from the New International Version Copyright ©1973, 1978, 1984, 2011 by Biblica, Inc.® Used by permission. All rights reserved worldwide.

Scripture References noted (KJV) were taken from The Holy Bible, King James Version. Cambridge Edition: 1769; King James Bible Online, 2015. www.kingjamesbibleonline.org

Printed in the United States of America
First printing, 2015

ISBN 978-0-9970655-0-3

Success Preferred / Media
PO BOX 116611
Carrollton, TX 75011-6611

Book Cover & Interior Design By:
Ruth Jones
Let's Go! Creative
www.LetsGoCreative.com

Dedication

This book is dedicated to the memory of Barbara Ann Fuller (Bobbie), my sister-friend since elementary school.
She was always my greatest encourager and cheerleader.
May she rest in the peace and arms of Jesus.
I look forward to seeing her again someday.

Sisters of the Heart

My heart and my mind still question
Why she had to go away,
But, there's peace and joy in knowing
I'll see my friend again someday.
There were so many little endearing things
That set her worlds apart.
For we were not merely friends, you see,
We were **Sisters of the Heart.**
She had her way of bringing out
The best in you and me.
One of her gifts was seeing those qualities
That others might not see.
She loved her work with children
And helping others to succeed.
When God gave her an assignment,
Barbara was ready and willing to lead.
Such a great aunt, sister, and friend,
We still can't believe it's true!
But, the Lord needed her at home.
He called her away from me and you.
Still hers was a life to celebrate,
And she didn't waste a minute.
Regardless of the task assigned,
She put her whole heart in it.

So I'll say goodbye to Bobbie now,
But only for awhile,
As she walks the streets of Heaven
Greeting others with her smile.
So even though she's gone from here,
And we're now worlds apart,
We'll always have that special bond
As Sisters of the Heart.

With Love, Felecia

"Poetry is when an emotion has found its thought and the thought has found words."
-Robert Frost

Contents

Foreword — xiii

Acknowledgements — xv

Introduction — xvii

Part I: To Encourage Your Spirit — 1

Lord, This Is How I See You	2
His Arms Are Open for You	3
As Hearts and Hands We Raise	5
You're Never Too Lost to be Found	7
When Trials Come	8
Just the Right Words	10
Focus on Being the Best You	11
My Beautiful One	13
Pockets Full of Possibilities	16
The Making of a Joyful Mother	19
Celebrate My Life	21
I'm Taking it Back	23

Part II: To Enlighten Your Thoughts   27

I'll Start With Me   29

Here I Am Again Lord   31

When God Bestows His Favor   32

Just Forgive and Let it Go   33

Who Is That Praying for You?   34

No Time Left   35

Maybe Tomorrow   37

Mind Your Business   38

Part III: To Entertain You   41

Who Is That in the Mirror?   43

Where Is He Lord?   45

When a Man Gives the Key to His Heart   46

Let Others Wonder Why   47

Been There, Done That!   49

Get Out of My Face!   50

Reality TV   52

I Don't Think So!   53

The Lady Biker Rides   55

Foreword

In my opinion, one of the most misused and undervalued words is "friend." It is more than a word; it is a "title" and should not be taken as lightly as many do.

As the journey of life will at some point reveal, a friend is so much more than a person with whom you "hang." A friend is more than a person you have known for years. A friend is a "safe place," an unconditional supporter. A friend honestly and compassionately tells you when you are not doing your best. Instead of judging you, she or he will encourage you toward greatness. A friend is a champion. Instead of walking away from you during your toughest life moments, a real friend throws you a buoy when a levee in your world breaks and sends you reeling and feeling overtaken. Ultimately, a friend is a gift from God.

> **Felecia Okpagu is the personification of a treasured, authentic friend.**

Although Felecia and I were members of the same church, we first met more than a decade ago when she became a charter member of "Write Now." I was blessed to serve as the group's inaugural leader for several years. Write Now, which began with more than 20 participants, eventually became a band of about six seasoned writers committed to encouraging each other's writing gifts and endeavors. This group of writers soon emerged as friends, creating a God-ordained sisterhood based on unconditional, supportive love. In addition to her continued involvement with Write Now, Felecia formed a new group, "The Write Direction," after a growing number of newer writers expressed interest in developing their crafts. She continues in that role today.

Felecia's undeniable writing gift is poetry. The same, genuine compassion she gives in her role as "friend," is heard and felt in every verse in her newest poetry collection, "Sometimes The Heart Must Speak." A true friend sometimes knows what you want to say even when you are unable to articulate it. That is what Felecia does through her uninhibited poetic expression. When you peruse the pages of this book, you are bound to find Felecia's reflections on real-life subject matter heartwarming, empowering, and in many cases, comforting.

Her heart for God and her heart for others are evident in her poetry. I am honored to call Felecia a friend and this book will likely have you calling her your friend too. Despite the depth of the challenges you face—whether in love, health, career, or life in general—there is nothing like having a friend to encourage you. "Sometimes The Heart Must Speak" is poetic friendship. For those of you who haven't yet met my friend, Ladies and Gentlemen, I'm proud to introduce you to a passionate, gifted poet, the author of "Sometimes The Heart Must Speak," my friend—and soon-to-be-yours—Felecia Okpagu.

Tracey New
Writer/Journalist/Blogger

Acknowledgements

First, I must express my love and honor for my Lord and Savior. He has been my guide through each word, each page, and every phase of this book. I am so humbled that He chose me to reach out to His people in this way. I cannot begin to tell you how much He means to me and how much I wish the same for you.

A very special thank you to Earma Brown, leader of the first writers group I joined. She was also the creator of my first author's website several years ago. This beginning helped to set the course for me and my writing. Thank you Earma!

I also have several wonderful friends who have come along beside me in walking through this process. That includes, my sisters from "Write Now" and "The Write Direction" writing groups. They have been true blessings in my life, creating for me a clear understanding of the phrase "iron sharpens iron." Also, thank you to Tonya Wilborn, Lauren Stevens, Jocelyn Stevens and Yvonne Free, who served as a part of my initial editing team. Ladies, you are fantastic! Special thanks to Carole Shannon, Kim Webb and Shuronda Scott for allowing me the honor of writing a poem based on each of their books. For Ms. Tracey New, I appreciate you so much girl! Not only for your contribution of the "Foreword" and back cover copy, but also for your creative ideas and suggestions. For my new friend, Ruth Jones of "Let's Go Creative," thank you for your design skills used in creating and designing the cover and interior of this book. Your enthusiasm is contagious. I felt you were right in there with me when it came to preparing a quality product that would bless those who read it. Thank you, so much. Finally, thank you to family and friends who encouraged me along the way. Your support means so much more than you will ever know.

In my opinion, there is no way to do justice to expressing how you feel about everyone in a short message like this. My hope is that you realize how your contributions have given me the encouragement and support needed to walk this path. Again, I thank you.

Introduction

How often in the course of just going about your daily life do you encounter news stories, events, people, negative thoughts, or feelings that totally overload your senses?

I usually turn on the news in the morning before work just to check the weather and traffic conditions, but sometimes all of the negative news from the night before just starts my day off in a not-so-positive light. Seldom do they have genuine "feel good" stories on there. Those would not be quite as news worthy, of course. It is so sad to see how our world has declined in morals, values, and just plain care and respect for one another. We certainly cannot live in a vacuum or stay inside locked away from the world, can we? Therefore, we watch and listen, perhaps voice our indignation, and try to put it aside and move on with life. Of course, each one of us has our own personal issues that we deal with, whether it is financial, job related, health issues, parenting, relationships, and the list goes on.

How do we deal with it? Well, for me, my faith and trust in God gets me through all situations. Otherwise, life would leave little hope. He gives me peace in the midst of all the struggles. I pray in the mornings for His guidance and throughout my day, and I am good to go. I cannot help but wonder how those who do not have that relationship are able to deal with the difficulties of life.

My desire in writing this book is to share some of the thoughts that started in my head and now reside in my heart. God gave me the gift of writing, and I want to use that gift to bless and inspire others. I have not written this book in judgment or as a sermon. Written here are thoughts and words to encourage, comfort, and provoke thoughts. My hope is that they also bring you an occasional smile.

PART I

To Encourage Your Spirit

Lord, This Is How I See You

In the silence I hear you speak,
Not out loud, not through my ears,
But deep down in my spirit.
Your words guide me and comfort me
As I face the everyday stresses and struggles
That this life brings forth.
When I retreat inside myself for comfort,
You are always there.
My needs are always met, whether they be
Emotional, as they frequently are,
Spiritual, more often than I can say,
Or physical, as my body ages and reacts to the
Strain of poor maintenance in my youth.
You're always there to wipe away the tears,
Calm the fears and give comfort during lonely times.
You are that beacon of light that guides me to safety
During the stormy times of my life,
And the problem solver, who always has the solution.
You provide the peace that lulls me to sleep at night
And the ray of sunshine that awakens me in the morning.
My heavenly Father, my Friend, my
provider, my Savior, **This Is How I See You.**

Proverbs 3:5-6 (NIV)
"Trust in the LORD with all your heart and lean not on your own understanding;
in all your ways submit to him, and he will make your paths straight."

His Arms Are Open for You

If my words should bring you comfort
And that peace you could not find,
It's because they're from our Father,
And He has you on His mind.
He sees what you've been going through,
And He wanted me to say,
He's waiting for an invitation
Into your heart someday.
But, you're one of those who finds it hard
To give up full control.
You want to be the one "in charge"
If the real truth should be told.
Still, now you seem to find yourself
In a dark and scary place.
The doctor gives you little hope.
There's fear etched in his face.
But, God says don't you worry now,
For He has the upper hand.
Your doctor has much knowledge, yes,
But, remember he's "just a man."
So when you feel you have no peace,
And your hope is missing too,
Try putting your faith in the Living God,
His arms are open for you.

A Note From the Author

I cannot help but feel a special excitement when I think of an opportunity for worship and praise to our Father in Heaven! It's such a special time shared with the church family. I wrote this poem as a testament to that feeling of anticipation of being in His presence. I love to look around and see others with their hands raised in the air as they worship. Of course, I am not so naive to think that everyone has the same experience or reactions. There can be distractions that cause your mind to wander. Mine has wandered on occasion. Still, I do believe that each person who engages in sincere worship experiences his or her own personal connection with Him.

When I hear complaints about the musicians, the singers, the songs, the arrangement of the songs, etc., I realize just how often we forget whom the worship is for in the first place. It is not for you or me, and it has little, if anything, to do with our pleasure. I am like everyone else in this situation. Some songs I love to hear and sing, but others not as much. We all love the familiar and being entertained. But, in those instances, I have learned to listen to the words and remember the purpose of our praise. Is He enjoying this? Do the voices filled with praise and worship bring a smile to His face? I believe the answer would be "Yes"! Even if you can't carry a tune, just make a joyful noise in sincere worship, and I believe it touches the heart of God. I have learned to take my personal need for entertainment out of the way. It is not about me. It is all about Him. So, I raise my voice (and my hands many times) to make a praise-filled, joyful noise unto the Lord!

Psalms 150:6 (NIV)
"Let everything that has breath praise the Lord. Praise the Lord."

As Hearts and Hands We Raise

When you enter the sanctuary
There's excitement all around
As we sit, anticipating,
Patiently waiting for the sound.
When the music starts to play
In love and honor we arise,
Giving praise to God our Father,
The One all knowing and all wise.
We go deeply into worship
With our hands up in the air.
You can feel the Father's presence
All around us everywhere.
If you haven't had the experience,
I pray someday soon, you will.
Just enter with sincerity.
Let your whole heart be filled.
For all the honor He deserves
In addition to all the praise.
We glorify Him with our worship
As hearts and hands, we raise.

A Note From the Author

Do you wish you had a huge eraser to go back and erase parts of your past? Do you feel that you have done such terrible things that you could never receive forgiveness? Have you lost hope? Not one of us is perfect, and we all carry guilty feelings about something. But, we have a loving and forgiving God who is ready and willing to forgive. We just have to go to Him in all sincerity and repent of our sins, asking for His forgiveness. He knows our weaknesses. Yet His love for us is so strong that He sent His own son to stand in our place and take our punishment. Then, we might have a chance to be saved. Still, we have free will, so each of us must seek Him for ourselves. Family and friends can only encourage you and pray. The relationship you form with Him will have to be personal.

I have heard so many testimonials of people buried in sinful behavior for years. Then one day something happened that turned them around. They invited Jesus into their hearts. You're never too lost to be found!

You're Never Too Lost to be Found

You're never too far down to get up,
But, you're the one who must believe.
God has the answer to every question.
You must ask Him to receive.

You're never much too lost to be found.
Stop thinking there is no hope for you.
He can lift you out of the darkness,
Or, He will stay there and walk you through.

You feel your sins are far too many,
And you're now lost for eternity?
Not one of us deserves His favor and grace,
But, He gives freely to you and me.

If you find yourself in a valley right now
In deep despair as you wonder about,
Seek the Lord. Ask Him to meet you there.
Then He will show you the way out.

When Trials Come

There are times in life when trials come
To teach you a thing or two.
It might even seem to be unfair,
But hold on, God has plans for you.
Don't be hard headed and self assured
Thinking only you know what's best.
If you'll just be still, listen and obey,
He will handle all the rest.
It might be sickness or financial woes
That will bring you to your knees,
But remember, God is in control.
Everything that goes on, He sees.
I have learned a lot through experience in life,
And I have cried a tear or two,
But I have never once doubted His love for me,
No matter what I had to walk through.
Those trials and tribulations came,
But I realized when they were gone,
They had instilled new knowledge in me,
While they also made me strong.
He knows just what we are capable of
And the size of the load we can bear.
Just remember, many times those struggles
Come to teach us and prepare.

So, remember the next time there are trials,
And you're lost in fear and doubt,
Take time to have a conversation with God.
Ask Him what this lesson's about.
Is He trying to teach you to trust Him,
Because He knows what is best for you?
Maybe He's showing that in faith, there is hope,
That He will always see you through.

Just the Right Words

The phrase "Thank You" is certainly gracious,
And it's used by most of us.
But for all the things our Father does,
I'm sorry, but it's not enough!
Yes, I use the term quite frequently,
And I'm sure that is true of you.
But, when I take the time to think about it,
A simple "Thank You" just won't do.
For now, I guess I have no choice
But to use what is available to me.
So "I Thank You Lord" with
My whole heart and with all sincerity.

Focus on Being the Best You

Do not try to imitate or join in all the debates
Of what the media declares to be true.
They rate the best body size and the best car to drive.
You just focus on being the best you.

Don't worry about things your friends might own,
Because yours is used, but theirs are brand new.
Who knows the price they paid for those things.
You just focus on being the best you.

If you can't afford their travel plans
Taking fun trips as they do,
Start saving and make your own plans,
But for now, just be awesome as you.

There are many who spend their entire lives
Trying to fit in and be accepted,
And they miss the beauty and pleasure in life
Because of fear in being rejected.

You are blessed and wonderful as you are,
But, you must know for yourself that it's true.
Otherwise, life will pass you by
When you could have enjoyed being you.

A Note From the Author

Prayer for the Beautiful One

Father, please bless the wonderful
lady reading this right now. Let her
recognize the qualities and gifts that You
have placed in her that make
her a blessing to those who know and
love her. Father I pray that she lets the
light of your spirit and your love shine
forever through her so that others
see a glimpse of You whenever she is around.
My biggest hope is that she will begin to see
herself as You see her, your **"Beautiful One."**

Proverbs 31:30 (NIV)
"Charm is deceptive, and beauty is fleeting;
but a woman who fears the LORD is to be praised."

My Beautiful One

My daughter, my precious and Beautiful One,
How special you are to my heart.
In love you were fashioned with intricate care.
From the start, I have set you apart.

With a Master's touch, and the Artist's eye
Not one thing was left undone.
You child are my greatest creation,
My cherished and Beautiful One.

I have given you hands that bring comfort,
And eyes that can see to the soul.
To your smile, I added special warmth
That can comfort the young and the old.

I instilled an inner knowing in you
To assist you with those in your care.
A voice that calms and a heart that loves
With an inner strength that is rare.

I know you have made mistakes in life.
My heart breaks when these things I see.
But, with open arms I wait for you.
Just repent, and return to me.

You child were created with purpose.
I have great plans for your life.
And yes, troubles may sometimes come,
But, fear not in times of strife.

If you follow me, I will lead the way
Until time for this life is done.
But, always know how special you are.
You're my precious and Beautiful One.

A Note From Shuronda Scott

When I was writing my book, "A Pocketful of Possibilities: Impossible Dreams Made Possible," one of the things I realized is that as a culture we have lost our ability to dream. There is no longer an aspiration, nor the inspiration to dream and to believe for great things. That is why the beauty and creative flow of poetry is so important. In the simple verses of a poem, we are encouraged and reminded, many times by just one word or one phrase, of the greatness and the goodness of our God.

Felecia's poem, "Pockets Full of Possibilities," based on my book, is a beautiful reminder of the deep pockets of God's amazing love and grace for our lives. It shows how much He loves us and desires great things for us, and yes, even the fulfillment of every dream. As scripture declares, "How high it is...how deep it is to know the love of God" (Eph 3:20). God wants to reveal His plan for your dreams and He wants to release you and give you the ability to step into them today. Let the inspiration of Felecia's beautiful poems spark the creativity to awaken the pockets full of hidden dreams for your life and that of others.

Shuronda Scott, Author
"A Pocketful of Possibilities: Impossible Dreams Made Possible"

Pockets Full of Possibilities

How could you doubt? How could you wonder?
He is the Master of <u>all</u> things.
Your dreams are certainly no challenge for The Lord.
He is Provider of "Impossible Dreams"...

Let your faith just move you forward.
Believe in all that your heart sees.
Our God is mighty and He is able,
With "Pockets full of Possibilities."

If you're in doubt and your heart falters
Due to your own inabilities,
Just trust and pray, and send praise upward,
His "Pockets are full of Possibilities."

We often limit ourselves and our dreams fall short
When we don't stand on His word and believe.
If He says, "Done" that is all that matters.
For Him there is no "Impossible Dream."

He'll give you beauty for those ashes,
Exposing greatness in you and me.
Don't hesitate to stand, believing.
You'll be amazed at the things you achieve.

In my own life, I've seen it happen,
Not just one time or even two,
When the impossible was made possible,
And yes, He'll do the same for you.

So let's all dream a dream together
Of how much better this life can be.
Stop delaying and procrastinating,
And dream of all the possibilities.

Inspired by the book "A Pocketful of Possibilities: Impossible Dreams Made Possible" by Shuronda Scott

A Note From the Author

Kim Webb shares her struggles with you in her book, "The Making of a Joyful Mother: A Spiritual Journey for Women Experiencing Infertility." She is transparent in her story, because her focus is on empowering other women who may be dealing with this now or in the future.

It was my honor to write the following poem, based on Kim's book. There is a powerful message on standing in faith and believing, even when you are in the midst of deep pain, doubt, and fears. Best of all, there is a happy ending!

Proverbs 23: 24-26 (NIV)
"The father of a righteous child has great joy; a man who fathers a wise son rejoices in him. May your father and mother rejoice; may she who gave you birth be joyful!"

The Making of a Joyful Mother

For years through heartfelt prayers
I cried to my Father up above,
"Lord please grant me your blessing,
And give me a child to love."

I had suffered through the physical pain.
I cried a million tears,
But, still my arms were empty
As the months turned into years.

The anger and the hurt I felt
Made it hard for me to see
That throughout all my trials in life
God had been right there for me.

I searched the scriptures, fell on my knees
And went to Him in prayer.
I felt His loving presence
As He waited for me there.

With faith renewed, I was content
With whatever He had for me.
My prayers were answered when I was told
"You're now a mom-to-be."

This child of ours is such a joy.
Our lives are truly blessed.
From this, I learned to stand in faith.
He will handle all the rest.

I love Him, and I trust Him.
For me, there is no other.
God already knew the plans He had
For "The Making of a Joyful Mother."

Inspired by the book "The Making of a Joyful Mother"
by Kimberly Webb

Celebrate My Life

Celebrate my Life! Please don't cry for me.
Put a smile upon your face!
When the time comes for my final breath
I will be headed for a better place.

There will be no more discomfort,
And I will have no dread or fear.
The regret I'll have around that time
Will be leaving my loved ones here.

My Heavenly Father will be waiting for me
With His arms held open wide.
At last, I will face the one I love
Who was always at my side.

So, on that day please celebrate.
Don't waste your time with tears,
Because I'll be hugging dear ones
I have missed for all these years.

A Note from Carole Shannon

When I wrote the book, "Spiritual Identity Theft and God's Plan for Transformation," it was to provide insight and encouragement to my readers about the importance of knowing who they are and whose they are. I wanted to be a voice in the world that helps guide those in "identity crisis," to a place of overcoming all those things in their lives that cause them to feel uncertain and insecure during those times that life brings them their greatest challenges.

Felecia took my message on identity and so brilliantly wrote this poem, "I'm Taking It Back," which encapsulates the themes found in the book but in an easily accessible way. "I'm Taking It Back" is a war cry for anyone sick and tired of the devil messing with them, tormenting, and harassing them. It is a cry that acknowledges the spiritual gifts and talents that we have, and through her words, she puts the enemy on notice that he no longer has any power over them.

Her sassy tone and the rhythm of this poem will draw you in with each verse.

If you find yourself going through an identity crisis or just need to feel strong in your own life, you will want to keep this poem handy. You will find yourself standing taller and stronger every time you read it.

Enjoy!

Carole W. Shannon, Author
"Spiritual Identity Theft and God's Plan for Transformation"

I'm Taking it Back

Listen, I sure hope you can see
You have taken all you're going take from me.
For years I buckled beneath the strain,
Now I'm getting back up in Jesus name.

I will no longer listen as you criticize
And fill my head with doubts and lies.
Get away from me! I know you're to blame,
And I'm ready to battle in Jesus name.

Great spiritual gifts God placed in me
To form and shape my identity.
So from my destruction you'll gain no fame,
Cause I'm blessed and delivered in Jesus name.

Yes, so many tears and broken dreams,
And too many wasted years, it seems.
But, I know now who I'm meant to be,
And I've recovered the spirit God placed in me.

So many have suffered because of you.
Your eviction is too long overdue.
It's time for us to all realize
Just how God views us through His eyes.

You best get ready for relocation,
Because God has plans for my transformation.
My spiritual identity has been re-claimed,
And I'm spreading the word in Jesus name!

Inspired by the book "Spiritual Identity Theft and God's Plan for Transformation" by Carole Whitfield Shannon

What Does Your Heart Say?

PART II

To Enlighten Your Thoughts

A Note from the Author

Isn't it funny that we always seem to know exactly what someone else needs to do to improve? We offer advice on what they need to change and whom they should or should not be in relationship with. Of course, we have opinions on what they wear. How in the world do we find the time to handle our own business when we are so busy in everybody's life? Well, that's just it. We cannot! How many times have you heard someone say "In my opinion...?" There lies part of the problem. We all have opinions, and we love to share them whether it is our business or not. The fact is, many times, we have a similar issue in our own lives that we are criticizing in someone else. Remember the Bible passage that reads, "Why do you look at the speck of sawdust in your brother's eye and pay no attention to the plank in your own eye?" **Matthew 7:3 (NIV).** That passage is so true.

I wrote this poem as a reminder to myself to change certain habits in my own life. I decided to start inventory on myself and not be so quick to offer up my opinions or criticisms of someone else. It is not an easy thing, because as I said, we are full of opinions. We must learn to keep those unsolicited little nothings to ourselves. If asked for an honest opinion, we should give it in love, sincerity and confidence or not at all.

I'll Start With Me

We <u>all</u> need to make changes
To be what God wants us to be,
And after serious inventory,
I think I'll start with me.

Before I go passing judgment
On what someone else has done.
I will look into my own past.
It sure wasn't a perfect one.

Then when I go to open my mouth
To spread some news I have heard,
I'll stop and think of what gossip does
Before repeating a single word.

I can't judge and criticize you
Giving my thoughts and advice.
We all need to look in the mirror.
Before speaking, think it over twice.

I have a box full of past mistakes
And failures to sort through,
And I have learned many a lesson
On things I should never do.

So, before you voice your opinion
Telling someone else how to be.
You might want to do what I did.
I decided to start with me.

A Note from the Author

I cannot tell you how many times a day I have to say, "Lord I am so sorry, please forgive me" for something. Our human flesh gives us a lot to overcome. Still, we must learn to contend with all the worldly influences that we come up against each day. I mean, between the television, radio, and the influence of other people that we encounter daily, it's a constant battle! Have you seen some of the things on television these days? Still, that is no excuse for our actions. My goal is to represent my Heavenly Father to the best of my ability.

When you decide to become a Christian, that decision comes with making up your mind on what your beliefs and standards are. What is it that is non-negotiable for you? What are the things (and sometimes people and places) that you will have to cut out of your life? Are you ready to carry yourself in such a manner that others know immediately that you are a Christian? I would be so ashamed if I told a co-worker or a new acquaintance that I was a Christian, and they looked completely shocked and said, "Really?" That would not only mean total embarrassment for me, but also that I have plenty of work to do. Still, there is peace and comfort in knowing that our Heavenly Father is willing to forgive, if we go to Him and sincerely repent.

Here I Am Again Lord

Here I come pleading again Lord,
Begging for your forgiveness once more.
I made you a promise this morning,
But, I messed up, just like times before.
I promised to try and do better
With things that I say and I do,
But as soon as I get around others,
I've broken my promise to you.
On my way into work I face traffic, and
When somebody makes a wrong move,
That's when my thoughts and my actions
Become something you would not approve.
I try to steer clear of all gossip,
And I know passing judgment is wrong.
Then someone asks for my opinion,
And my tongue has a mind of its own.
Lord, I'm not here just giving excuses,
And I know I am fully to blame.
I am just asking you to be patient.
Help me these bad habits to change.
I know that I've caused you concern Lord.
I have been working on this for a while.
Still, I know when I ask I'm forgiven.
I know you still call me your child.

When God Bestows His Favor

When God bestows on you His favor
Be very grateful, but stay prepared
For the possible slings and arrows
From those who think it is not fair.

True friends will always be happy for you
And any blessings you might receive.
False friends find you undeserving,
But, may not express what they believe.

You might notice in their actions
That they don't treat you quite the same.
Do not let it hurt or bother you
It is their issue. You are not to blame.

Somehow you should always remember,
When God opens a door for you,
It is because He trusts you
To do what He needs you to do.

So honor that trust He has in you.
Don't you worry about what others say.
In fact, those friends who don't wish you well
Were not your good friends anyway.

Just Forgive and Let It Go

For years a spirit deep inside
Has destroyed peace in your soul.
You've allowed it space within your heart,
And it strengthens as you grow old.
Yes, I speak of what I choose to
Call the unforgiving heart.
Although it's buried deep inside
It is tearing your life apart.
Whatever the cause or reason
It's not worth the sacrifice.
It's costing you a chance for
Joy and happiness in your life.
A smile is foreign on your face.
There is no warmth in your voice.
You blame another for the state you are in,
But, you certainly have a choice.
Stop holding on to all those hurts
That happened years ago.
To bring God's peace into your life,
Just forgive it, and let it go.
Now, I know you say I was not there
To see what you went through.
That may be true, but I do see
The effect it has had on you.

Who Is That Praying for You?

I have heard it said often, and I believe it's true,
That you don't want just anybody praying for you.
Some will quote Bible passages they may have read,
But, they don't seem to show faith in what was said.

Then along comes another who may offer a prayer,
But, when they open their mouth, there's no substance there.
Still, others use great big words to impress
Just to gain more attention for them, I guess.

What you want is someone who leaves no doubt
That they know what Faith in God is all about.
It is certainly not using impressive words,
But when their prayers go up, you feel for sure they are heard.

Now that's certainly not meant to exclude you.
You need a one on one with the Father, too.
If someone is praying and you have a choice,
Just make sure God will recognize the voice.

No Time Left

If you knew tomorrow was your last day on earth
Just how different would your life today be?
Would you show more love and compassion
To those folks you may no longer see?

Would that include showing forgiveness
For those who have caused you offense?
Now would considering the needs of others
Seem to suddenly make more sense?

Somehow, I cannot help but wonder,
As I question these things for myself,
Are most folks waiting to make those changes
When they think there is no time left?

A Note From the Author

On the news the other day, I heard a reporter talking about a family who had a terrible car accident on the way to their much-anticipated vacation. There were eight family members in the car and five of them died! What a horrible tragedy! One minute everyone is enjoying the trip and excited about their destination, and in an instant, that all changed. It brings home the fact that we just never know when our time here on earth will be over. That is what I was thinking when I wrote this poem. Tomorrow is not promised, and neither is later today. Still, I think the younger you are, the harder it is to imagine that you will not be around for a very long time. No one received such a guarantee. That is why it is so important that we decide today whom we will serve. God certainly does not force us to accept Him. It is up to the individual. Many times worldly distractions keep us unfocused. Others sometimes have too much influence over us, especially when we are younger.

My message is simple: We make time for everything else in our lives that we consider important. Have you added The Lord to your schedule? Are you waiting until tomorrow?

Maybe Tomorrow

"Maybe tomorrow" is what you told her
When she started to share *The Word*.
You just had no time to listen,
Besides, it's boring you had heard.
"Maybe next time" was your answer
About Sunday Service to attend.
You have other plans on that day,
And you love just sleeping in.
"Ask me later," when the question came
About "What do you believe?"
You had never thought about it.
He just gives, and you receive.
Why do all these "Jesus" people
Seem to keep on bugging you?
What do they care if you know Him?
That should be left up to you.
You still felt that as a young man
You had much time to decide.
Someday soon, you'd think about it,
But, for now, you would let it slide.
Then one early Saturday evening
As you sped down that highway,
You just had no way of knowing
Your tomorrow….was today.

Mind Your Business

You told everybody what you had heard
Without verifying a single word.
Now you find that it was all absurd.
You need to just *Mind Your Business.*

You wonder, "Why does she dress like that,
With those too-tight jeans and that ugly hat?"
And it looks to me like she's getting fat!
You need to just *Mind Your Business.*

You were wondering how he got that car
Since he's a night waiter at some bar.
You've heard how low their wages are.
You need to just *Mind Your Business.*

Now, even if these things were true
They still have nothing to do with you.
Think about it, and you know it's true.
You need to just *Mind Your Business.*

You know you're guilty and so am I.
We look at others with a critical eye.
We all have issues, you can't deny.
It's best to just *Mind Your Business.*

What Does Your Heart Say?

PART III

To Entertain You

A Note from the Author

We are always our own worse critics. It seems that the problem is more prevalent in females, but men do it too. I guess it is a little mixture of pride and insecurity. By that, I mean pride in who you are makes you want to look your best and always put your best foot forward when being around others. Yet, there is that side of us that is always just a little insecure, especially as we start to age. We start to see changes in our skin, physical body, hair, or eyes, and we forget how wonderfully we are created. God has given each of us a uniqueness all our own. I have seen many celebrities, both men and women, who had plastic surgery to try to maintain that youthful beauty that once made them so proud and confident. Many times the results did not satisfy. A few died due to unforeseen complications. Still, that does not deter those in search of eternal youth and beauty.

This poem is just a comical reminder of how harshly we judge ourselves.

1 Samuel 16:7 (NIV)
"The LORD does not look at the things people look at. People look at the outward appearance, but the LORD looks at the heart."

Who Is That in the Mirror?

I am sure you have noticed in your mirror,
And I have seen them in mine too,
Many glaring imperfections,
That are mainly seen by you.

A wrinkle here, a pimple there,
Growing bigger with each minute.
You hate to face the mirror,
Because who knows what you'll see in it.

Hips too big, and waist too thick
They're right there staring at you.
Surely, everyone else can see,
But they just won't say it's true.

Nose too wide or lips too thin,
They have to be improved.
Then there's that tiny mole right there.
That has to be removed!

Hair is dull and much too dry,
Now you're starting to see gray in it.
Good thing you can buy hair now
To improve on things a bit.

Just too loud, or maybe too quiet,
There's just no fixing you.
Not very smart or just too brainy,
Whatever will you do?

Stop right now, and think about it,
And a minute is all it takes.
God is the creator of us all.
And He never makes mistakes.

Where Is He Lord?

That special man created just for me,
Who will share my heart for eternity,
I haven't met him yet, because the times not right.
Now, I'm a patient woman, but **Where is he Lord?**

He will be my "soul mate," no doubt about it.
For my life, he will be the perfect fit.
The time and place only the good Lord knows.
I'm just preparing myself, so **Where is he Lord?**

Unconditional love is what I'm looking for,
And of course, he's someone that I'll adore.
But, I'm getting older, and I'm starting to wonder,
Is my list too long? Then **Where is he Lord?**

Now I joke about the situation,
But, I trust in the Master of all Creation.
I know that when it is meant to be,
He has the perfect one for me.

In the meantime, I'll just be content,
And enjoy being free of entanglement.
Some say I don't know how good I've got it.
I'd like to test that theory, so **Where is he Lord?**

When a Man Gives the Key to His Heart

He may not have the right words to say,
Or just the right thing to brighten your day.
That is not a talent God gave him,
But, you have the key to his heart.

Don't expect long speeches with loving words,
And giving flowers, to him, seems a little absurd,
But, you're still most definitely the one, you see,
So, cherish that key to his heart.

Romantic evenings with dancing and such,
To him, seems just a little too much.
He's content to sit home and watch TV,
But still, to his heart, you alone hold the key.

So, he may not make the greatest impression
Cause he's not very good at true love expression,
But don't ever doubt his sincerity
When he gives you the key to his heart.

Let Others Wonder Why

I close my eyes and there you are
To brighten up my day.
If this life lasts a thousand years,
I will always feel this way.

You have this way of saying things
That speak right to my heart.
Whenever I'm angry, you make me laugh
Before the fight can start.

Romance, passion, thoughtfulness,
I could never ask for more.
That's why each day, I love you,
Even more than the day before.

We have had our fights. I must admit
There were some heated ones.
But, there is fun in making up
After all the yelling is done.

No one is ever perfect.
We know this, you and I.
We've found what seems to work for us.
Let others wonder why.

A Note from the Author

Can you relate to the following poem? I believe most of us can. We have all had relationships that we knew were toxic for us. Still, for some strange reason we held on. That goes for both men and women. In some cases, we have convinced ourselves that this person is the soul mate we have been searching for, and we have the magic formula to change them.

I was in a relationship, quite a few years ago now, with a person that I thought was "Mr. All That." He always made me feel so special. When we were together all of his attention was on me, and he called several times a day. He was not bad to look at either. Of course, "Mr. All That" always knew just the right things to say. He was always very affectionate and very respectful (or so I thought). Well, apparently I was sleepwalking, because for a time, I was just not paying attention to any "red flags" that came up.

One day my eyes were opened when I found out that "Mr. All That" had married a girlfriend he had been with for years! Of course, he had never mentioned her before! There was no sign of another relationship. He lived in a small town outside of where I lived, so that made it easy to hide the fact. To make matters worse, he didn't tell me this news himself. I found out from a friend of his, who could not contain the secret any longer. At any rate, he had several lies to tell in trying to form his defense. Our relationship ended, of course. He kept calling, but my eyes had been opened. That was not in God's plan for me.

We have all "Been There, Done That!" Now, I use that life lesson to make me much wiser and more discerning. What about you?

Been There, Done That!

Hey Girl! Come on and get a clue,
Stop crying because that man walked out on you!
If he couldn't treat you with a little respect,
This could be the best thing that he's done yet.
You say he calls you terrible names,
And he's a pro at lying and playing games.
So what are you trying to hold on to?
We all deserve respect, and so do you.
I try to mind my business, but from where I stand,
You deserve better quality in your man.
God designed a woman like a gem that is rare.
Each one should be loved and handled with care.
Don't you roll your eyes over here at me
As if I have no clue or authority!
"I've been there, done that, got that t-shirt too!"
So I understand more than you think I do.
Now, you say you'll do what you think is best.
From you friend, I'd expect nothing less.
You can pursue this man who deceives and neglects,
And never seems to treat you with any respect.
I pray he will become what you want him to be,
But, in the meantime, please don't complain to me.

Get Out of My Face!

Man, you best get out of my face!
I don't even care to know your name.
You seem to have all the right things to say,
But, I can see right through your game.

Now you say you have a wife at home
While you're a player out trying to be.
If that is the life you want to live,
That's fine, but don't include me.

I neither want nor need such drama,
And the Bible calls adultery a sin.
I am trying to live the best I can,
And that does not include a married man.

Now, I will admit you have a certain charm
That tends to work on some, I'm sure,
But for me, I imagine the pain and the heartache
Your poor wife must endure.

It's really sad that since the world began
Some folks never seem content.
They have eighty-percent in the spouse at home,
But, they still want that other twenty percent.

So why not do yourself a big favor,
And go on home to your family.
You may say no, and that's your choice,
But, please stay away from me.

Luke 18:20 (KJV)
"Thou knowest the commandments, Do not commit adultery, Do not kill, Do not steal, Do not bear false witness, Honour thy father and thy mother."

Reality TV

Would someone please explain to me
The huge popularity of reality TV?
That's where someone's life is on display
As cameras, follow them throughout their day.

Just how in the world could you be persuaded
To let all of your privacy be invaded?
The phrase "Money talks" I guess is true.
It's amazing the things it will make some do.

I have read news reports of marriages ended
And reputations that cannot be mended.
Still, I guess if the public did not support
The producers of such would soon abort.

They are "like a train wreck!" I heard someone say.
"If you start to watch, it's hard to turn away."
So, keep on watching, if you must,
But, what in the world does that say about us?

Mark 8:36 (KJV)
"For what shall it profit a man, if he shall gain the whole world, and lose his own soul?"

I Don't Think So!

Satan, why do you keep messing with me?
You should have given up long ago.
I know your plan is to destroy or distract me,
But, listen up, **"I Don't Think So!"**

You've caused me pain and many sorrows,
That sometimes brought my feelings low.
Then I prayed and renewed my spirit,
So hear me now, **"I Don't Think So!"**

It seems you've been quite busy lately
With all the things that are going on.
I would think you'd have quite enough to do,
So, you could just leave me alone.

But, since that's not very likely to happen
I'd like to just make sure you know,
That you can try your best to bring me down,
But, read my lips, **"I Don't Think So!"**

A Note from the Author

Just close your eyes and picture this "Lady Biker" whizzing by on her Harley! I actually wrote this in honor of a friend and mentor of mine. She was a consult through my church. For recreation, she rode with a group of friends on the weekends. They took little road trips occasionally.

I would describe her as a business executive, church leader, mentor, and awesome woman of God who enjoys riding her bike. I was truly amazed to see this huge, yellow Harley! Those things look so much smaller at a distance! I truly appreciate her. She helped me to listen to hear the voice of God when searching for answers. In the process, I also received a lot of great encouragement and advice, and we became great friends. She lives miles away now, but I wrote this poem out of gratitude and respect.

The Lady Biker Rides

She loves the taste of freedom
As over the winding road she glides.
With amazing skills and confidence
The lady biker rides.
Do not try to classify her.
There is nothing typical here.
Just step aside as she goes by,
And it's best that you stand clear.
With the wind in her face, she deeply inhales,
As the road ahead unwinds.
All of life's stresses are gone and forgotten
As this Lady Biker rides.
Don't refer to her as a "biker chick."
She does not fit into that mold.
She is a tall, blond-haired executive,
With a heart of solid gold.
She never travels all alone,
Because Jesus is at her side.
He has also surrounded her with angels
Disguised as friends who ride.
For me she was a mentor
When my vision was not clear.
She taught me how to listen
So that God's voice I might hear.

As she passes, don't just stop and stare
With your mouth held open wide.
Just give her the utmost of respect,
When this Lady Biker rides.

What Does Your Heart Say?

Notes

1. A very special "Thank You!" to Carole Shannon for her contribution of the introductory remarks to "I'm Taking it Back!", which was inspired by her book, **"Spiritual Identity Theft and God's Plan for Transformation,"** copyright © 2008 by Carole Whitfield Shannon.

2. A very special "Thank You!" to Shuronda Scott for her contribution of the introductory remarks to "Pockets Full of Possibilities," which was inspired by her book, **"A Pocketful of Possibilities: Impossible Dreams Made Possible,"** copyright © 2012 by Shuronda Scott.

3. Opening quotation by Robert Frost is available in the public domain.

4. Back cover copy is courtesy of Writer/Journalist/Blogger, Tracey New. Blog site: scrapeyourplate.wordpress.com.

Special Order Poems

Framed copies or bookmarks of any poem in this collection may be special ordered by contacting the author. If that is your desire, please **email Contact@AuthorFeleciaO.com** for more information on pricing and delivery options. Also, for a free price quote, please state all information pertaining to the poem requested, frame size (if applicable), and desired quantity.

FRAMED ART

BOOKMARKS

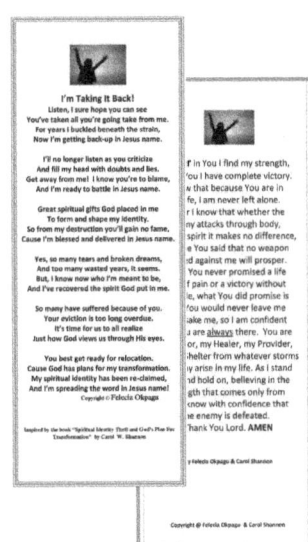

Visit me on the Web:

www.AuthorFeleciaO.com
Email: Contact@AuthorFeleciaO.com
www.facebook.com/AuthorFeleciaOkpagu
LinkedIn: Felecia Okpagu

About the Author

Felecia Okpagu has more than 20 years of corporate experience in the area of Billing/Finance. Prior to that, she worked several years as a licensed optician with both small and large corporations. Her experience as a writer began as more of a hobby or side interest many years ago. During that time, she self published and sold her first book of poetry, "Through My Eyes," online. In addition, she started a small part-time business, "Feleciawrites," creating customized poetry for all types of occasions.

In the meantime, Felecia had become a member of a Small Group Ministry of women writers through her church. The first group was lead by Earma Brown and served to increase her interest in developing her writing gift. After this group disbanded, she became one of the charter members of a second Small Group Ministry called "Write Now." This group of supportive Christian sisters, led by Tracey New, was influential in helping her to move toward her writing goals and developing the gift God had given.

As interest in the writers' group increased, there was a need for a second group. In 2008, Felecia was appointed, by her church, as leader of the new Small Group Ministry, "The Write Direction," and she still leads that group today. Through this group, she has been able to provide resources and learning opportunities to beginning women writers. Presently, she is working closely with the current leader of "Write Now," Carole Shannon, to formulate an environment for writers to grow and flourish in their writing.

All of this has lead Felecia to this point and this book. She has a heart for God and reaching His people with those messages He has placed in her heart. Felecia's feeling is that in the "Army of The Lord" writers serve a huge role and have great responsibility in these times of turmoil. God uses many methods to reach His people, and writing is one of them.

Connect with Felecia:

www.AuthorFeleciaO.com
Email: Contact@AuthorFeleciaO.com
www.facebook.com/AuthorFeleciaOkpagu
LinkedIn: Felecia Okpagu

www.ingramcontent.com/pod-product-compliance
Lightning Source LLC
Chambersburg PA
CBHW031416040426
42444CB00005B/593